THE ROLE OF LITERATURE IN READING INSTRUCTION
CROSS-CULTURAL VIEWS

Dorothy S. Strickland, Editor
Teachers College Columbia University
New York, New York
United States of America

ira

Selected Papers, Part 2
Seventh IRA World Congress on Reading
Hamburg, August 1-3, 1978
Dorothy S. Strickland, Chairperson and Series Editor

International Reading Association
800 Barksdale Road
Newark, Delaware   United States of America

Copyright 1981 by the
International Reading Association, Inc.

Library of Congress Cataloging in Publication Data
World Congress on Reading, 7th, Hamburg, 1978.
  The role of literature in reading instruction.
Selected Papers, Part 2, Seventh IRA World
Congress on Reading, Hamburg, August 1-3, 1978,
Dorothy S. Strickland, Chairperson and Series Editor.
  Includes bibliographies.
  1. Children—Books and reading—Congresses.
I. Strickland, Dorothy S. II. International
Reading Association. III. Title.
Z1037.A1W65   1978   372.4'1   80-26794
ISBN 0-87207-429-3

372.41
W89r
119725
new.1981

Contents

Foreword

The Role of Literature in Reading Instruction: Cross-Cultural Views is the second volume in a series of three titles selected from papers read at the Seventh IRA World Congress on Reading in Hamburg, Germany, in August 1978. Dorothy S. Strickland, then President of the Association, and Chairperson of the Congress, is Series Editor.

In offering this book to its membership and to others concerned with the promotion of literacy throughout the world, the International Reading Association presents a powerful statement of conditions which must be met for optimal learning and for maintenance of the reading habit.

Each paper is, in itself, substantive and thought provoking. The combination of papers sets off echoes and awakens inferences as one reads, so that the facets of meaning flash and reveal themselves while possible solutions to problems begin to unfold in the reader's mind. Why not this? Why not that?

A number of slim books have moved their readers to shape history by improving the human condition. It is in this sense, that of starting readers to think and act and involve others, that this book will prove its power and we the readers, our constructive, creative, global worth.

Philip Morrison of MIT, commenting on the nature of civilization in a televised lecture, "Termites and Telescopes," said that termites would never in the length of time left to the universe change their architecture; alter their habit of eating injured fellow workers; or learn to speed up their work with language, written records, and mathematics. Although we, too, have all the time in the world, human misery stemming from illiteracy can't wait. Human beings must be in a hurry.

Perhaps if we concentrate on solutions to our problems, we shall see who is useful for what, and how a little assistance will sweeten us all.

If literature is to attest humanity's efforts toward a better world, quality literature must be selected, translated if necessary, and transported. Its coming must be heralded by all means and media, so that when it arrives it will receive the welcome and usage it deserves.

Ways for it to be displayed and used should be modeled and taught to the adults in the home, school, and community who are the teachers and to the children who teach each other. For lifelong learning, children and adults must be shown how to learn, how to teach themselves, and how to think.

The beautiful books now produced in many countries for the pleasure and cultural development of children are variously priced according to the cost of production and other considerations, but some inexpensive books are beautiful and excellent in their content. Paperbacks are cheaper to mail and easier to handle.

Some books are said to travel well. This is said of the poems and essays of the famous Argentine writer, Jorge Luis Borges. The meaning of *travel* in this context, however, has to do with the universal appeal of his ideas. Borges has said that a reader is also a writer. Different readers take to an author's material the meanings their experiences dictate. This is a priceless characteristic for successful readers.

But the right of readers to interpret meanings according to their own cultures causes havoc when the readers are professional translators overly confident in their task. The very confidence which made them readers in the first place now plays them false.

In spite of these difficulties, let it be acknowledged that many translators and interpreters are receiving excellent special training sponsored by their governments. Not only do they direct their attention to the possible meanings of words and larger units within the context of the original language and purpose of the author, they also take precautions in the selection of words and explanatory aids and illustrations for the target language.

What if the target language has no written form? Around the world, linguists are busily coding the spoken language into graphic forms. Teachers trained in linguistics help children write their own stories and poems in their own language so that, for the first time, the children see the equivalent of their speech in written form. Their parents both teach and learn with them to the extent that they are free to do so.

How are books transported to readers in remote places? In Nepal they may come by aerial cable, as do the fruits and vegetables from milder climates and lower elevations; they may be dropped by helicopter; or they may arrive by plane when roads are impassable. For delivery to nomadic tribes, such as those following reindeer herds in Lapland, a bookmobile or sled-mounted library classroom trails the procession.

Somewhat the reverse of this plan of bringing the books to the remote area is the Thai-Hilltribes Foundation plan at The Farm in Chiengrai. Villagers accompanied by their children take turns traveling down to Chiengrai. There at a special school they learn to produce salable items from their own traditional handcrafts and extend their knowledge of good health habits and agriculture. As nomads they could deplete the fertility of the soil and move every few years to another place. But now that land is in more demand, it is time to learn more economical ways of maintaining and cultivating what they have. This project is one of the many charities of the Princess Mother (the King's Mother).

Some tribes had a taboo against reading because it kept the reader from socializing while others danced and chatted and played games and sang in free time. Nor was anyone to read, for goodness' sake, when every able-bodied person was working simply to survive. Reading is more sociable now on the model farm in Chiengrai. With their own hands and many of their own ideas, the hill people have built a reading room next to the school. Association members and others have sent books and given financial support to the reading room. Nakorn Pongnoi, an IRA member, has been the on-site developer of the reading room for the Princess Mother, continuing his responsibility for the entire farm plan, a notable one for educators.

In the United States, schools are the most vital channels for the spreading of literature. Among the exceptional educators who have devoted themselves to readers and literature is May Hill Arbuthnot who spent most of her middle and later years teaching children's literature at the Western Reserve University in Cleveland. Her influence lives on in her many publications.

Educators have worried about television as a competitor of literature, but today we have plenty of evidence of its support on memorable occasions. Recently, Station KQED of the Public Broadcasting System presented a program produced by Beverly Ornstein which is soon to be available in transcript and perhaps videotape from the Far West Institute (3231 Pierce Street, San Francisco, CA 94123). The speaker and storyteller was Laurens VanderPost, the South African collector of traditional stories around the world.

Van der Post said it is the same everywhere when people have to leave their homes for one reason or another. It isn't so much the home that they miss or the land. It's the stories that come in the wind in the place they lived, where they knew who they were and where they were going.

In one story of the First People of the Kalihari—that is, those first human beings to live and hunt there—there was an aged hunter. A hunter is very important in that desert land, for if he doesn't find game for his people, they go hungry. If he has bad luck for many days, they may even starve. For years he had hunted for their food, especially hoping to kill a great white bird. Now he was aged and exhausted from his search, but he still felt impelled to follow the bird. Not to kill it.

Catching a glimpse of it from the corner of his eye, he thought he could be at peace if only he could touch it, but it had flown somewhere ahead. Just then, a sheer wall of rock rising to a cliff far above his reach blocked his ascent and stopped him short. There was the great white bird on the cliff.

The hunter, drained of strength, lay on the ground beneath the high cliff. But as he lay dying, a white feather dropped down beside his hand. He grasped it with joy and died happy.

In the modern world of work and logic and separation of families from their roots and homes for whatever reason, there seems to be no room for one's touch with mystery. But people need to be in touch with something they can believe in and hold to. They yearn for a truth that transforms. Some people even become deranged by its denial.

A therapy is said to be found in the nonrational and curative forms of art—storytelling from old cultures, dancing, and singing of the music brought on the wind. This loss of meaning in existence is everywhere in the collective unconscious.

The above notes paraphrase not too well what Van der Post said movingly that day. The faces of his listeners were beautiful with their involvement. If descendants of the First People had indeed been in the auditorium, could they have been identified by an appearance of greater involvement?

Congratulations to the readers of this foreword on being about to read a most stimulating and significant publication whose editors and authors are distinguished leaders in their fields. Good company!

Introduction

The papers included in this collection were originally presented at the Seventh International Reading Association World Congress on Reading which was held in Hamburg, Germany, in August 1978. The authors focus on cross-cultural concerns related to literature and literacy. In the first paper, Helen Huus discusses the development of the field of children's literature as a separate field of study. Huus describes the emerging interest in children's literature as reflected throughout the world in libraries and library collections, at exhibits and book fairs, at professional conferences and seminars, in professional literature, and in teacher education programs as a preservice requirement or elective and as a topic for graduate research.

Zena Sutherland explores the many problems connected with the translation of books for children. Problems involving the selection of books, the quality of translation, and the difficulty in reviewing such books are described. Despite the numerous difficulties, Sutherland stresses the importance of making books from all countries available to all children in order to help them understand and appreciate the cultural diversity of our world.

Takeshi Izumoji's report on the use of children's literature in early childhood education in Japan is based on the research results of the Child Education Research Department of the Tokyo Municipal Education Research Institute. Izumoji describes how literature is used in the school setting to support the social and cognitive development of young children.

In the final paper, Ralph Staiger focuses on what various countries around the world are doing to promote the reading habit among school children and the general citizenry. Book promotion projects and programs designed to develop worthwhile reading tastes and a permanent interest in reading are described. According to Staiger, we have a responsibility to go beyond teaching individuals *how* to read to insure the development and appreciation of the value of reading in a democratic society.

DSS

Literature for Children:
An Emerging Discipline Internationally

Helen Huus
University of Missouri
Kansas City, Missouri
United States of America

"Literature," according to one dictionary, is "writings in prose or poetry...having excellence of form or universal interest related to man." Literature for children includes such writings prepared especially for them, plus writings they have appropriated as their own. It includes those literary works children can read for themselves or can understand at their levels of maturity. Literature for children is part of the ongoing stream of literature in general and, as such, deserves the same recognition, dignity, and serious study as that accorded any field of literature.

A "discipline" is "a branch of instruction or education," and while children's books have been published for centuries, literature for children, as a branch of instruction or separate field of study comparable to that of Renaissance Literature or The Modern Novel, has been slow to evolve.

Upon analysis, four stages become apparent in the development of any new discipline: 1) the creation of a unique body of knowledge, 2) the establishment of standards, 3) recognition by peers and colleagues, and 4) acceptance by the academic world. These stages are not discrete and not completely sequential, for activities overlap between stages and some developments occur simultaneously. Nevertheless, all elements are necessary in the process.

The Body of Knowledge

The development of a unique body of children's literature at the international level is dependent in part upon what is done nationally. The establishment of libraries and special collections, the publication of professional books, and the mounting of exhibits all allow a country's literature for children to be viewed as a whole.

Libraries and collections

Libraries like the International Youth Library in Munich provide an international overview. This library was founded in 1949 by Jella Lepman, who was self-exiled from Germany and became a British citizen. After World War II, she returned to her homeland and, because she had a deep and abiding conviction that children throughout the world must develop true understanding of one another and that this could be effected through children's books, she developed the IYL. The Library is now an associated project of UNESCO and houses approximately 200,000 volumes in about 50 languages, including the complete book collection of the International Bureau of Education in Geneva. Publishers around the world send their productions free of charge in order to keep the collection up-to-date.

Another international collection of children's books is maintained in New York City at the United Nations International Children's Educational Fund (UNICEF) Information Center on Children's Cultures. Other libraries and centers often include a limited number of foreign books; for example, the Osborne, Lillian H. Smith, and Canadian Collections in Toronto, Canada and the Institute for the Intellectual Development of Children and Young Adults in Tehran, Iran.

Several countries support documentation centers that house their complete production of children's books. Among these are Centro Diddatico Nationale di Studi e Documentazione in Florence, Italy; the Educational Materials Review Center (EDMARC) in Washington, D.C.; and La Joie par les Livres in Paris, France. The year's production of English books can be seen at the National Book League in London and, if present plans materialize, Dromkeen Homestead (near Riddell, Victoria) eventually will serve as a documentation center for Australia.

(Dromkeen was purchased in 1973 by Court and Joyce Oldmeadow and first opened in October 1974. At present, the collection contains approximately 1,500 Australian children's books, several hundred original illustrations, manuscripts, and artist's mock-ups. In 1976, the Oldmeadows received the Eleanor Farjeon Award for their contributions to children's literature, the first time the award had been given to someone outside of England.)

Specialized collections like those of the Grimm Museum in Kassel, Germany; of Hans Christian Andersen's works in Odense, Denmark; of the Johanna Spyri Foundation in Zurich; and of the Pinocchio Monument in Collodi, Italy, also provide material for study and comparison.

Professional books

Books that organize the field of children's literature have helped define the body of knowledge—books like May Hill Arbuthnot's original *Children and Books*, which stood alone in America for so many years or, more recently, John Rowe Townsend's *Written for Children: An Outline of English Language Children's Literature.*

Books that trace the historical development in an area or a country also contribute. Among these are Bettina Hürlimann's *Three Centuries of Children's Books in Europe*; the works of Marcus Crouch, Frank Eyre, and Percy Muir in England; Cornelia Meigs and others in the United States; Sonja Hagemann in Norway; Eva von Zweigbergk and Mary Ørvig in Sweden; and H.M. Saxby in Australia. Iceland, Denmark, Germany, and other countries have similar historical accounts which provide the serious student with a perspective of the field.

Exhibits and fairs

While the transient nature of fairs, exhibits, and festivals prohibits prolonged study, they do provide sources of up-to-date information and an opportunity for cross-national comparisons, and their published catalogs have utility for those who cannot attend in person.

The Children's Book Fair in Bologna, Italy, each April and the fall Frankfurt Book Fair allow representatives of many countries to display children's books of the past year and offer an opportunity for editors and publishers to become acquainted, compare notes, and negotiate exchanges and translations.

The International Book Festival in Nice, France, sponsored by the City of Nice, was first held in 1975 on the theme "I can read...and after?" And the Biennale of Illustrations Bratislava (Czechoslovakia), which is held in odd-numbered years, attracts beautiful books from both East and West.

Approximately ten exhibits per year are sent on tour by the IYL. These present an international view of a specific theme, the best books from one country, or the complete works of an author or illustrator of international renown.

Collections, professional books, and exhibits all help create the corpus of literature for children at the international level. A definitive account of the international scene, however, is yet to come.

The Establishment of Standards

The second stage in development is the establishment of standards, and a regular plan for writing and sharing critiques must be established. Conferences and seminars where books are discussed and evaluated, journals that carry critical reviews, and the distribution of annotated lists of recommended books are ways that call attention to the best books and, through the critiques, set up standards of quality.

Conferences and seminars

International conferences and seminars offer opportunities for presenting critical studies; for discussing standards; and for meeting authors, illustrators, booksellers, publishers, and others interested in producing good children's books. Perhaps the best known of these meetings is the annual Loughborough International Seminar on Children's Literature. The Loughborough Technical College Library School in West Bridgeford, England, sponsors the seminar, held each year in a different country with registration limited to insure international representation.

The International Institute for Children's Literature and Reading Research, based in Vienna, Austria, holds an annual conference, usually in an attractive setting outside the city. The International Board on Books for Young People (IBBY) holds congresses biennially. Recent congresses were held in Rio de Janiero in 1974, in Athens in 1976, and in Würzburg, Germany, in 1978. The Boston Public Library sponsors an annual symposium on Children's Books International.

The Australian National Section of IBBY conducted a 1978 conference at Sydney University on the theme, "Through Folklore to Literature." Speakers from England, Germany, Japan, New Guinea, and the United States participated, giving the meeting an international flavor.

Other activities in the Pacific area include the Pacific Rim Conference on Children's Literature, first held in Vancouver, British Columbia, Canada, in May 1976. The first Arctic Rim Children's Literature Congress convened in Barrow, Alaska, in June 1977. Only children's literature specialists from countries bordering on the Arctic Ocean were allowed to register, although some outsiders were invited to present papers or to observe. Also in 1977, the Upper Yangtze River Children's Literature Exchange in the People's Republic of China conducted a conference in honor of the forty-fifth anniversary of the publication of Elizabeth Foreman Lewis' *Young Fu of the Upper Yangtze.*

In 1978, the Latin American Seminar on Children's Literature was held in Rio de Janiero on the theme, "Realism and Reality in Latin American Children's Literature." Also in 1978, the first International Conference on Children's Literature in Spanish was convened in San Francisco, California, jointly sponsored by the Bay Area Bilingual Education League (BABEL) and the University of San Francisco.

These conferences and seminars provide a forum for the discussion and evaluation of children's books, which ultimately influences the development of standards and the upgrading of quality.

Journals

Only a few journals treat literature for children on the international level, though national journals often carry information from other countries.

Bookbird, now in its eighteenth year, is a joint publication of IBBY and the International Institute for Children's Literature and Reading Research (Vienna). It contains critical reviews of children's books, articles on the status of juvenile literature in various countries, information on authors and illustrators, and discussions of recurrent themes in children's books. It also presents a calendar of events, news from the National Sections of IBBY, bibliographies of professional literature, suggestions of books for translation, and lists of awards.

Children's Literature in Education: An International Quarterly began in 1970 and for its first three years was published three times a year in London. In 1973, publication was moved to New York; in 1975, the journal became a quarterly. It is confined to reports relating to the children's book world, primarily in England and America, and articles treat topics similar to those in *Bookbird,* plus an occasional research report.

Phaedrus: An International Journal of Children's Literature Research, which was started as a Newsletter in 1973, is issued twice a year and contains research, reports, and extensive bibliographies of special interest to researchers and college teachers of literature. Recent themed issues dealt with juvenile literature in the USSR, periodicals for children, and the state of television in several countries.

Although national journals like the American *Horn Book,* the Australian *Reading Time,* and the Norwegian *Bokbladet* sometimes contain articles on international themes, their main purpose is to consider their nation's publications. Moreover, language barriers limit the usefulness of journals. Not enough exchange is currently available among continents other than Europe, America, and the English speaking world, but hopeful signs are on the horizon for South America and Africa.

Critical articles, critiques of books, and discussions of criteria provide an opportunity for individuals to compare their evaluations with those of their counterparts in other countries. As books cross international lines and meet the critics from other cultures, they stand or fall on their universal qualities.

Awards

International awards stimulate the production of books of high quality by recognizing superior books in international competition. Foremost are two Hans Christian Andersen Awards—one for literary merit, first presented in 1956 to Eleanor Farjeon of England for her complete works, and one for illustration, first given to Alois Carigiet of Switzerland in 1966. The IRA annual Children's Book Award recognizes a new writer's first or second book from any country in any language. Laurence Yep's *Dragonwings* won the first award in 1976. The Mildred Batchelder Award, presented annually since 1968 to the "American publisher of the best juvenile book originally published abroad in another language and subsequently translated into English," has international implications in the selection of books to be translated, and two awards for illustration are presented at the Bratislava Biennale—the Grand Prix and the Golden Apple. Two prizes are awarded at the Bologna Book Fair—the Fiera di Bologna Graphic Prize for the best children's and juvenile book and the Critici in Erba Prize for the best illustrated book selected by a jury of children; the International Book Award, first given in 1975 by the International Book Committee, is for "outstanding services rendered by a person or an institution to the cause of books."

Conferences and seminars, journals and awards all stimulate discussion and evaluation of the literature for children and thus contribute to the development of standards of quality on an international level.

Recognition by Peers and Colleagues

The third requisite in the development of a discipline is recognition by peers and colleagues. On some American college campuses, the basic course in literature for children has been dubbed "Kiddie Lit," which does little to enhance its image as a serious study. Professional colleagues in other departments sometimes react negatively when children's literature is mentioned; nevertheless, acquainting others (including the general public) with the field is a significant activity.

Organizations

International organizations lend support in creating a favorable image, and it is comforting to find others of like mind who believe in the importance of good books for the young.

Foremost at the international level is IBBY, which was started in 1953 as a dream of Jella Lepman. She called a meeting of children's book specialists throughout the world, and the International Board on Books for Young People was born as a forum for the exchange of ideas and experiences. The organization is made up of National Sections in America, South America, and both East and West Europe, but not completely yet in Africa and Asia. The Sections are composed of public institutions, organizations, and individuals interested in promoting children's books. Since 1976, Friends of IBBY groups have been formed, thus extending the personal involvement of members.

Other international organizations like the International Federation of Library Associations (IFLA), UNESCO, UNICEF, and the World Confederation of Organizations of the Teaching Profession (WCOTP) support and promote children's books internationally in conjunction with their other projects. The International Reading Association, through its membership in UNESCO's International Book Committee (formed in 1973), its World Congresses, and its annual Book Award, also provides vehicles for international exchange and recognition. The Franklin Books Program, a nonprofit organization, promotes book publishing in Asia, Africa, and Latin America. It concentrates on translating and publishing materials in the local languages and stimulates native writers.

In addition to library and educational associations, groups of "book people" have also formed local and national literature associations which support the international effort and lend prestige to the field. While these may begin modestly, their influence often gains momentum—as in the case of the Children's Literature Association of New Zealand, which now has eight branches with well over a thousand members, including some from overseas. Japan has a Children's Book Association; the Philippines, a group called PAMANA; and the United States, a Children's Literature Assembly (an affiliate of the National Council of Teachers of English) and a Children's

Huus

Literature Association, connected with the Modern Language Association. These organizations keep their members informed about new books and other developments in the field and circulate information to the general public.

Still another source of international information is provided by the various children's literature tours sponsored by universities or associations. This combination of study and travel has widened the horizons of teachers, librarians, and parents as they hear writers and artists speak and see libraries, research centers, and authors' homes (for example Beatrix Potter's in Near Sawrey, England).

The media also disseminates information about children's books. France has a weekly television program entitled, "Books for You," in addition to a weekly radio program based on books for children. In New Zealand and Denmark, occasional television programs review children's books, interview authors and illustrators, and present discussions. Sweden has a series of programs; and one of the courses on "Sunrise Semester" in the United States dealt with children's books and reading. Newspapers and periodicals in several countries carry book reviews on occasion; France has five specialized and nine general journals that carry reviews and articles.

Other types of activities include a seminar for parents sponsored by the Institute for the Intellectual Development of Children and Young Adults in Tehran, and the book promotion program of the National Council of Cultural Affairs in Sweden, which involves 100 titles of 1,000 copies each, organized into packets on 18 different themes to be used with youth organizations. In addition, lists of recommended books, sometimes with annotations, are prepared regularly by groups such as the Schools Library Service in New Zealand, the documentation center in Paris, the Swedish libraries central service organization, the National Book League in London, and the Society for Children's Literature (Schweitzerische Bund für Jugendliteratur) in Switzerland.

All this activity by organizations and the media informs not only those who work with children but the general public as well. And as people become informed, a recognition of the importance of literature in the lives of children and young people is likely to follow.

Acceptance by the Academic World

The fourth element in the development of a discipline is acceptance by the academic world. Required literature courses in the preparation of elementary school teachers, the establishment of research centers, and the sponsoring of research studies by universities are all indications that juvenile literature is becoming accepted as a legitimate field of study.

Teacher education

In the United States, many colleges and universities offer at least one course in literature for children as part of the teacher preparation program, but not all states require it for elementary teaching certification.

In England, most teacher training institutions offer some studies and all teachers' colleges in Sweden include children's literature in their education. The University of Stockholm offers an interdisciplinary course on "Children's Cultures" and the State School for Library Education, the Swedish Library Association, and the Swedish Institute for Children's Books all arrange courses at one time or another.

In Denmark, two of the universities offer courses, but most of the work in children's literature is given at the Royal Danish School of Educational Studies and Denmark's Library School. A few courses in children's literature have been offered recently at the University of Geneva. In Poland, a course is obligatory for students of Polish philology, pedagogics, and preschool education.

Australian teacher training colleges and technical institutes as well as the College of Advanced Education offer courses and, in New Zealand, all eight teachers' colleges provide lengthy courses in children's literature. Most of the colleges cooperate with neighboring universities in establishing B.Ed. degrees with children's literature as a degree paper.

These few reports indicate a growing trend toward the inclusion of courses in children's literature at teachers' colleges and some universities. However, until literature for children is accepted generally by the universities in any given country, can it rightly be characterized a "discipline"?

Research centers

An exciting and relatively recent development is the establishment of research centers for children's literature. The Institute for Youth Book Research was founded in 1963 at the University of Frankfurt, where each semester 400-600 students are enrolled. Doctoral studies have treated such topics as "Gangs and Cliques in Children's Books," "Discussions about a Proletarian Children's Literature within the History of the Workers' Movement," and "Fairy Tales as Educational Instruments—The Changing Theoretical Positions in the 19th and 20th Centuries." Some research takes a pedagogical direction; some studies are historical-descriptive; some analyze the ideological content; and others treat various genres.

The Swedish Institute for Children's Books, which was opened to the public in 1967, serves as a documentation and information center for children's books. In 1975, the collection contained approximately 20,500 Swedish children's books, nearly 3,100 reference works on international literature, and approximately 70 periodicals. Several studies have been published by the Institute, exhibits have been arranged, consultant services have been provided for those planning seminars and conferences, and courses have been arranged cooperatively with other organizations.

To date, the activities at Dromkeen (the National Centre for Children's Literature in Australia) have focused on making books come alive for children. As many as 300 children have attended a storytelling session, and other activities include puppet shows, visiting authors and illustrators, and special speakers. While Dromkeen has not yet been used very much for serious research, students are beginning to work with its collection of Australian material.

The French Information and Documentation Center on Children's Literature conducts research in children's books and also publishes a children's literature journal.

New research centers established within the past few years include the Centre for Children's Literature at the University of Haifa, the Center for the Study of Children's Literature at Simmons College in Boston (with support from the National Endowment for the Humanities), and the Children's Book Research Information Centre at the University of Wales Institute of Science and Technology at Cardiff. Still another is the Center for the Book in the Library of Congress, which held its first seminar in April 1978 on the topic, "Television, the Book, and the Classroom."

Although some of these centers and institutes also serve as documentation centers, their chief function is to sponsor, conduct, and report research. Their activities have lent considerable prestige to the field and, in some countries, have helped literature for children achieve a status approaching that of adult literature.

University research

During the past ten years, research on literature for children has greatly increased at universities in the United States, as attested by the bibliographies published regularly in *Phaedrus*. In 1976, IRA issued an annotated bibliography, *Research in Children's Literature*, which included studies completed between 1960 and 1974. However, much of the research remains on university shelves, unavailable for want of publication.

Germany has a long history of research on juvenile literature, as does the USSR. In other countries, research at universities is just beginning; for example, the University of Oslo in Norway, the University of Zurich, Massey University at Palmerston North, and Auckland University, New Zealand.

Research organizations

In 1970, the International Research Society was established, with its registration in Frankfurt, Germany. Its purposes are to further research in literature, reading, and related fields for children and youth; to provide exchange of information and discussion of theoretical questions; and, where possible, to coordinate research activities. Membership is obtainable only on a personal basis and is granted by the Board. As of January 1978, the nearly 200 members came from 32 countries. Completed studies reported by members include the content and illustration of children's books, book distribution practices, and the reading of literature in the comprehensive school. This society offers an opportunity for cross-national studies as researchers from different countries correspond and consider projects of general interest.

The increasing acceptance of literature for children by the academic world is indicated by the inclusion of courses in teachers' colleges and universities, by the establishment of research centers which are sometimes university based, and by the increasing number of doctoral studies. The new research society provides the possibility for true international cooperation, but its work has just begun.

Conclusion

This discussion has focused on four stages in the development of literature for children as it progresses toward becoming an international discipline. The past decade has seen enormous progress, at both national and international levels, and the future looks bright. The challenge now is to get on with the job.

Bibliography

1. "Action Line," *American Libraries*, 7 (September 1976), 496.
2. Alderson, Brian. "A Comment on Children's Literature," *Phaedrus*, 3 (Spring 1976), 30-31.
3. "Children's Books International Exhibition," *Bookbird*, 13 (1976), 55.
4. Children's Literature Association, *Yearbook 1977*. Auckland, New Zealand: Children's Literature Association, North Shore Teachers College.
5. Crago, Hugh, and Maureen Crago. "Children's Literature Research: A Bibliographic Essay," *Phaedrus*, 3 (Spring 1976), 26-27.
6. Doderer, Klaus. "A Few Comments on Children's Literature Research in the Federal Republic of Germany," *Phaedrus*, 2 (Fall 1975), 5-7.
7. Donovan, John. "Conference Notes from All Over," *School Library Journal*, 24 (November 1977), 22-26.
8. *Dromkeen: A Home for Australian Children's Literature*. Riddells Creek, Victoria: Dromkeen Children's Literature Foundation, 1977.
9. "First International Book Award," *Bookbird*, 13 (1975), 61.
10. Furuland, Lars. "A Swedish Project on Children's Literature," *Phaedrus*, 2 (Spring 1975), 10.
11. Gilderdale, Betty. "New Zealand," *Phaedrus*, 3 (Fall 1976), 31-32.
12. Haviland, Virginia. "International Book Awards and other Celebrations of Distinction," *Bookbird*, 14 (1976), 11-20.
13. Hoyle, Karen Nelson. "International Projects at the Kerlan Collection," *Bookbird*, 13 (1976), 19-29.
14. Humbert, Genevieve. "France," *Phaedrus*, 5 (Spring 1978), 49-50.
15. IBBY. *The Calendar*, 36 (November 1977-June 1978).

16. "The International Research Society for Children's Literature," *Phaedrus*, 1 (Fall 1973), 3.
17. Kirk, Heather. "The Osborne Collection of Early Children's Books," *Bookbird*, 13 (1976), 29-34.
18. Motyashov, Igor. "Children's Literature Research in the Soviet Union," *Phaedrus*, 4 (Spring 1977), 29-30.
19. Pellowski, Anne. "Internationalism in Children's Literature," in Zena Sutherland and May Hill Arbuthnot (Eds.), *Children and Books*. Glenview, Illinois: Scott, Foresman, 1977, 615-619.
20. *Phaedrus*, 4 (Fall 1977). Issue on Children's Periodicals.
21. Ray, Sheila G. "Institutions and Organisations for Children's Literature: The British Situation," *Bookbird*, 15 (1977), 10-13.
22. Roth, Edith Brill. "A First and Only Treasure," *American Education*, 13 (November 1977), 6-9.
23. "Twelfth Children's Book Fair in Bologna," *Bookbird*, 13 (1975), 61.
24. U.S. Section, Friends of IBBY *Newsletter*, 3 (Summer-Fall 1978), 5-17. (Mimeographed)
25. U.S. Section, Friends of IBBY *Newsletter*, 3 (Winter-Spring 1977-1978), 8-19. (Mimeographed)

The Problems of Translating Children's Books

Zena Sutherland
University of Chicago
Chicago, Illinois
United States of America

It is very easy to be lyrical about the advantages of making books from all countries available to children, and the reason it is easy is that those advantages are so obvious. First, as adults dedicated to children's reading, we applaud cross-cultural enrichment and the dissemination of the best in children's literature; presumably it is the best that is translated and made a part of the world's literature available to children. Second, in a world in which increasing travel and rapidly expanding communications media bring people into closer contact than ever before, translated books enable children to understand and respect other cultural patterns, to empathize with children of other countries, and to see the universal qualities of life as well as the enthralling differences. Third, whether fiction or nonfiction, books about other countries give factual information; and such information is usually more reliable than books written by outsiders about those countries. Such books also lack the patronizing tone that assumes a food or custom other than one's own is quaint, exotic, or peculiar. Fourth, books from another country may be of a kind or about a subject not available in one's own land. In sum, new horizons and new bonds are acquired.

But are the best books always translated? And how well are they translated? How are they chosen, and what problems do they present? How are they accepted? Who are the decision makers in the long process of searching for and finding what's to be translated? Who is responsible for rejecting or approving the translation process? Let us first examine the roles of the original authors, the editors who choose books for translation, and the translators.

The original author seldom has a voice in decisions about translations. Agreements are usually made between publishers, sometimes among several publishers, who propose a copublishing venture that will cut costs. Authors may have few rights, save for the fact that their permission is needed to make substantive changes, but they often have complaints. If the authors are familiar enough with the language to read translations of their books, it may be sadly evident that the translator has been inept or the editor careless. A letter I received from Spanish author Maria Luisa Gefaell de Vivanco in 1970, says the following:

> I feel deeply ashamed when I read the English, French, or Italian translations of my books. I have always been so painfully faithful when translating other people's books... that I cannot understand how the coeditors [an Italian publisher] can be so inconsiderate. I work so deep... seeking always a poetic and good language without rhetoric that I could cry as I see translations as the ones of [a United States publisher]. Where did... people find this translator, who does *not* know a bit of Spanish, and is capable of writing such enormous things as "the ladies were embroidering *helmets*" and calls again and again "Don Rodriquez" to "Don Rodrigo"... and does *not* translate but only "digest" in the worst way my books? I think that the United States are full of people who speak Spanish well. It should not have been difficult for the sirs [of the U.S. publisher] to find one who at the same time knew my language and a little history of literature.

Fortunately, Cervantes cannot see the sentence I found in a badly adapted version of *Don Quixote*: "Don mounted his horse and rode off..." nor Mark Twain see the copy of *The Prince and the Pauper* I bought in Spain, the cover and title page of which attribute the story to *Mack* Twain.

Of course such atrocities are not found in the majority of translated books, nor are they restricted to any country; they are cited to show the pitfalls in translation. Most editors (and translators) are conscientious and sensitive about the quality of translation. But what and how do they decide to translate? There is little question that editors look primarily for good books that lend themselves to smooth translation. If one examines the kinds of books chosen, it is clear that the majority are either books in the public domain (which includes most classics), books that have won prizes or received other favorable attention, series books, or books by authors who have already sold well in translation.

The avenues of access are diverse: Editors see books at special exhibits, at conferences, and at international book fairs; they read publications like *Bookbird* (published by the International Board on Books for Young People), especially noting prize winning books; they receive suggestions from translators or from friends in other countries; they rely heavily on personal visits and, once a relationship is established with an editor abroad, there may be agreements on future options or first refusal rights. If they are fortunate, editors may have an inhouse staff member who reads a foreign language, or they may have access to a foreign language bookstore. They watch reviews and bibliographies, and they consider suggestions from literary agents.

Once a tentative choice of a book has been made, the editor may ask several readers for an opinion as to the book's literary quality and its suitability for translation. Next there is the problem of choosing the translator. Lucky the editor who can turn to a translator of established and deservedly high reputation. Unlike the author, the translator will usually prepare the entire manuscript, which means a major investment of time for both translator and editor, for the editing of a translation can be a very time consuming process.

The specific function of the translator is to produce a version of the original work that will satisfy the editor and editorial advisors. "Traduttore, traditore," says the Italian maxim: To translate is to betray. Certainly the heart of the translation problem is to translate without betraying. What makes it possible for translators to do this? It may seem simplistic to say that they must know a second language thoroughly, but those embroidered helmets remind us that it is possible to publish a book in which that knowledge is lacking. Translation should always be from the second language to the native language so that translators can be at their most fluent and idiomatic. Translators must make language flow, must have a sense of style, must be able to write well—and they are far more likely to do this in their own language.

The most difficult problem is choosing the middle path between literal translation, which results in stiff and often awkward literal adherence to the original, and a translation so free that it loses all resemblance to the original and may lose the precision of detail that gives form, structure, and color to the book. The translator's obligation is to interpret the author with integrity; but to maintain that integrity, to preserve the linguistic equivalents of the author's story, intent, and style, means that the translator must be a channel, a sympathetic interpreter.

Patricia Crampton (2) says the translator "must be prepared, in fact it is his professional duty to prepare himself, to be totally immersed in the intentions as well as the style of the original author." This, Crampton notes, helps avoid oddities of dialogue. Regardless of familiarity with a second language, one must cope with several kinds of obstacles. Each language has its own pattern and cadence; what is poetic in one may be sentimental in another. It is harder to translate books for children than books for adults, since what may be a mild hazard for an adult may be an obdurate barrier for a child.

One such obstacle is practical: The translation of such things as terms of measurement, slang, currency, or titles for which there are no exact equivalents. A second is idiomatic— the interpretation of a colloquialism that, if literally translated, would lose or change meaning. A third is cultural. A story written in a country that has a single religious or political orientation may need amplification or editing to be comprehensible to readers in other countries. A fourth has to do with latent content, those references that are dependent on common knowledge or shared heritage. This is noticeable in allusions to childhood games and often is particularly acute in translating humor, when comprehension often rests on oblique reference as it does on an untranslatable pun on words.

Given all this, the translator must work slowly, seeking for the exact word and the sensitive phrase, checking to make sure there are no errors of fact or interpretation. And, since translators are paid by the word (more specifically, by a set fee per thousand words) it follows that the more conscientious— and therefore slow—the work, the less financially rewarding per hour, unless there is a royalty or bonus arrangement with the publisher.

When the translator's work is done, the editor faces a job that may be more difficult than editing an original manuscript. Editor Helen Wolff says, "I have seen a translation lauded as 'impeccable' in a trade journal, knowing that every page needed ten to twenty corrections.... This, of course, does not apply to a distinguished roster of names known to everyone in our profession.... Fat files of correspondence testify to their maniacal conscientiousness, their constant preoccupation with getting everything just right. They are meticulous and punctual.... They will insist on reading proofs (for which they are not remunerated). They have the professional pride of the foremost bullfighters" (2).

As to the reviewers, who also play a role in the fate of a translated book—how do they judge? Not having read the original, in most cases, they must evaluate the book they see. If it is possible to see the armature of the original language because of a literal rendering of phrase or an idiom, the book is weakened, for the translator's style, however good it may be in general, has at that point come between the reader and the author. If the dialogue doesn't have a natural flow, the reviewer may not know whether to attribute this to the author or to the translator, but the dialogue still is not convincing. Reviewers also judge on the amount or difficulty of material that, in their opinions, should have been translated. Certainly it is reasonable to expect, in an edition of an English book published in the United States, that an English child will say "lift" rather than "elevator." The context, however, should make clear what a lift is; it should not be necessary for the translator to introduce an explanation. That's an example of problems that arise when children share a common language. It's not necessary to change terms as much as it is to clarify them, and even that decision depends on context. If children of other countries don't know what sauerbraten is, it seems sufficient if it is made clear that it is a kind of food.

Problems can arise even within one country. Jamake Highwater (4), an American Indian, says in the preface to his book, "At the core of each person's life is a package of beliefs that he or she learns and that has been culturally determined long in advance of the person's birth. That is equally true for Indians and for white people. The world is made coherent by our description of it. Language permits us to express ourselves, but it also places limits on what we are able to say." How much more difficult it is for translators to create a bridge when the two languages with which they are working have little or nothing in common linguistically or culturally!

The reasons books are translated and the channels by which they may have been brought to an editor's attention have been mentioned, but one must keep in mind that publishing is a business. What's in it for the publisher? For one thing, diversity enhances the publisher's reputation; for another, most editors of children's books have a sincere interest in making it possible for children to have the best available literature. Yet they must keep financial strictures in mind; every house limits the number of books it publishes, and—especially in smaller houses and in smaller countries where the size of the potential readership is limited—each time an editor chooses to publish a translation, some other book will not be published. That's why such an editor may choose a book that's been popular in the original language rather than a book that has received a prize for literary quality but that clearly will appeal to a smaller group of readers than the popular book.

Alas, translated books seldom show an impressive profit. In the United States, bookstores which tend to stock mostly series, classics, winners of major prizes, and comparatively lightweight popular authors, seldom carry translated books. Less than 20 percent of the new books published each year are to be found in bookstores in the United States. And translated books are new books. Why take a risk? The present financial situation has affected translations as it has almost every aspect of publishing, not only in the cautious attitude of stores, but in the atrophied budgets of the prime consumers of children's trade books—the libraries.

Another limiting factor is cultural disparity. Children cannot absorb what they cannot understand. Faced with a reader's report that a book would be incomprehensible, it is the editor's decision to publish or not to publish. Or it may be that the problem is complexity of style. Pondering the fact that Virginia Hamilton was not published in Great Britain until she won the Newbery Award (although all her previous books had been well received), John Donovan (3) says, "The explanations for this reticence are very mystifying" and he quotes such phrases as "very American" and "language verging on the idiosyncratic." Yet there is no doubt that Hamilton is one of the great stylists writing for children today. (There is also the possibility that British editors had not felt there would be a responsive audience for black books in Great Britain.) Again, the book for the few may appeal to a corresponding few in any country; that doesn't lessen its literary worth, but a small audience increases financial risk and that means such a book is less likely to be purchased for translation.

Countries that publish few books may not be meeting all the reading needs of their children, so that editors seek books for translation to fill the gaps. While the primary consideration may be literary quality, an editor may well choose a book for its genre or the information it gives or the subject with which it deals in order to fill what the editor feels is an unmet need.

In addition to the facts that there is little support in bookstores for translated books, and that sales even to libraries (which constitute the major market for children's books, at least in the United States) are unimpressive, publishers may find that their profits are cut due to disadvantageous exchange rates. Mary Ørvig (6), discussing economic conditions in the publishing of Swedish children's books, points out that "Publishers have to concentrate more and more on established authors and reliable types of books." What this implies for the translated book is obvious.

Aase Bredsdorff (1) reporting on Danish publishing, notes that "... translations of cheap foreign series, for example The Golden Books, seriously hampered our own production of picture books which are, necessarily, more expensive because of the fewer copies printed." Bredsdorff goes on to comment that, in a country where picture books comprise the most valuable part of children's book production, this was catastrophic. (Valuable indeed, with two Danish artists who have won the Hans Christian Andersen Award!) Bredsdorff also deplores the fact that so few English language prize books are translated. This, in a country in which most translations (as is true for other Scandinavian countries) are from either other Scandinavian languages or English: in which the majority of children's books are translations; and in which, with limited publishing resources, "Every bad book excludes a good one."

In the same book (*Translation of Children's Books*),

Margaretha Schildt, editor at Bonniers, notes that editors are reluctant to try a book on faith but that often, after a book appears in translation in a major language, it will be picked up for translation by publishers in other countries. Their reluctance to take the initiative is based not only on the fact that translations may not be profitable but that they usually involve more work for editors, because of a higher potential for errors.

The whole procedure of translation, in sum, seems fraught with risks and problems for the overworked editor and the underpaid translator. Why bother? There are two good reasons: Books and children. All of us are concerned with children, with what and how they read, with the possibility that mediocre books contribute to reading reluctance, and with how reading may affect their lives; we are aware of the importance of making books from all countries available to all children. We want to help them become world citizens, to offer them not just some but all of the best in children's literature.

There have been many developments that tend to make these goals more attainable. There is the increased attention to children's books in international book fairs such as those at Leipzig or Frankfurt, the evolution of such special events as the annual children's book fair at Bologna or the Biennale of Illustrations Bratislava. There are such international centers as the International Youth Library in Munich or the Information Centre on Children's Cultures in New York as well as the many national centers that have international scope, such as the Children's Book Institute in Stockholm. There is IBBY (International Board on Books for Young People) and its very useful publication, *Bookbird*; and there are all the international activities of IBBY's national sections. There are lists of books recommended for translation (such as those published by the American Library Association) and there are ongoing projects in which books are chosen for donation to libraries in other countries, particularly in the emergent nations. There are the developing publishing industries in smaller countries, with such catalytic agencies as the Institute for the Intellectual Development of Children and Youth in Iran.

There is evidence of the growing recognition of the importance of the work of the translator in the establishment of such awards as the Mildred Batchelder Award for translation or the inclusion of translators on the list of Hans Christian Andersen honor books. There are the international Hans Christian Andersen Awards and the many national awards for which authors from other countries are eligible. There are increasing numbers of organisations like the International Reading Association that demonstrate concern for the child's book as a medium of cultural exchange as well as a shared literary heritage.

In addition to all these expanding areas, what more do we need? We need better press coverage of meetings; more prizes and other events in the children's book world; recognition by the larger literary world of the importance of children's literature; and bookstores that stock more and better children's books, including well-reviewed translations. We need more parent groups like the British "Books for Your Children" program, more emphasis on children's literature in training programs for librarians and teachers, stronger translators' associations, more editors who attended the book fairs at both Frankfurt and Leipzig, and recognition of the fact that improvements in any part of the children's book field can contribute to other parts as well as the whole. We should remember that large countries need cultural infusion as much as do small countries.

Jella Lepman (5), founder of the International Board on Books for Young People and of the International Youth Library, describing the early years of those institutions, says "In many parts of the world children were holding books in their hands and meeting over a bridge of children's books. And this was only a start." Despite all the problems inherent in translation, children's books are a mighty buttress for that bridge. And we see why when we look at the categories for the Special Hans Christian Andersen Honors List for 1979, the Year of the Child: international understanding, promoting concern for the disadvantaged and handicapped, human rights, getting to know one's own and other cultures, concern for the environment, and peace. While such concerns are manifest in the books of all countries, there is surely no better way to lead children toward international friendship and trust than to foster their understanding, through translated books, of the fact that such deep concerns are shared by children all over the world.

References

1. BREDSDORFF, AASE. "On the Problems of a Small Country Concerning the Translation of Children's Books," in Lisa-Christina Persson (Ed.), *Translation of Children's Books.* Bibliotekstjänst, Lund, Sweden: 1962.
2. CRAMPTON, PATRICIA. "Will It Travel Well?" *Signal*, 17 (May 1975), 75-80.
3. DONOVAN, JOHN. "American Dispatch," *Signal*, 17 (May 1975), 91-95.
4. HIGHWATER, JAMAKE. *Many Smokes, Many Moons.* New York: Lippincott, 1978.
5. LEPMAN, JELLA. *Die Kinderbuchbrücke.* Frankfurt: S. Fischer Verlag, 1964.
6. ØRVIG, MARY. "Children's Books in Translation: Facts and Beliefs," *School Library Journal*, 19 (November 1972), 23-27.
7. WOLFF, HELEN. "The Trials of Translation: The Publisher Speaks," *Publishers Weekly*, 204 (September 24, 1973), 120.

Sutherland

The Use of Picture Books for Education of Children in Kindergarten and Nursery School in Japan

Takeshi Izumoji
No. 4 Ochiai Municipal Elementary School
Shinjuku, Tokyo
Japan

Child Education in Japan

For purposes of this study, children were grouped into two categories—infancy (up to two years old) and preschool ages (between three and five).

A majority of Japanese infants are reared by their mothers at home. Recently, however, an increasing number of mothers in Japan have been leaving their children at day nurseries in order to work. Unfortunately, such day care facilities are not yet sufficient in this country. Japanese parents of children between three and five years of age tend to eagerly send them to kindergarten, chiefly for the education offered by such institutions.

About 64 percent (2,370,000) of those children between three and five years of age go to kindergarten. There are 130,000 three year olds; 980,000 four year olds; and 1,260,000 five year olds (as of May 1, 1976, based on the survey by the Ministry of Education). Thus, seven times as many four year olds as three year olds go to kindergarten, and about ten times as many five year olds, when compared with three year olds, attend such preschool institutions. This means that the older the child (and, thus, the closer to eligibility for compulsory education), the higher the percentage of enrollment in kindergarten in Japan.

This tendency is more pronounced in cities than in rural areas. For example, in Tokyo, 95 percent of five year olds, 88 percent of four year olds, and 26 percent of three year olds go to kindergartens and day nurseries. And almost all parents of four and five year olds, who haven't been admitted into such institutions earlier for various reasons, wish to send their children to kindergarten to make sure they receive proper child education before receiving compulsory education at elementary school. This trend will most likely continue and the desire of such parents for better child education will surely grow stronger in the future.

Interests among Japanese Parents in the Education of Their Children

Most Japanese parents are interested in the education of their children, which is indicated in part by their keen interest in picture books.

A survey on the attitudes of mothers toward picture books was conducted at six kindergartens in Tokyo, each involving different social and living environments. The 274 mothers of five year olds were asked to state their reasons for giving picture books to their children. It was found that many of these mothers do this simply for the purpose of child education.

Results of the survey show that Japanese mothers give their children picture books for the following reasons.

	Percentage
They want their children to find the joy of reading	81
They want them to be more creative and imaginative	66
They want them to be knowledgeable	52
They want them to learn words	25
They want them to become familiar with pictures	20
They want to use picture books to teach manners	20
They want to make the parent-child relationship better and more meaningful	19
Their children want picture books	18
Mothers, themselves, like picture books and want their children to read them	8

The order of the top three answers was the same at all kindergartens surveyed.

According to the same survey, 80 percent of the children have picture books read by their mothers at home. In addition, 12 percent of the children have picture books read by their mothers often, and only 8 percent answered that their mothers do not read picture books for them at home. This indicates that, through the positive efforts of their mothers, a majority of children are familiar with picture books before they go to kindergarten and day nursery.

Mental and Attitude Changes of Children in Group Situations

Mental and attitude changes of children in group situations over the period of one year can be divided into six steps.

The first step is the period when children are put in a new environment (kindergarten) and, feeling mentally insecure, gradually find for themselves a place to feel secure. This period is around April, the new school year in Japan.

The second step is the period when these children, having found what they can do in their new surroundings, try to approach others.

The third step is when the children become interested in their surroundings and begin to expand their activities.

After the summer vacation comes the so-called "recurrence period" in early September when children again feel a bit insecure and show the symptoms of the first step. However, they soon recover.

The fourth step is characterized by the children's preference of friends, games, and activities. They make full efforts in their activities.

In the fifth step, children develop positive attitudes to assist them in overcoming difficulties in their activities. During this period, they show interest in what is going on around them.

The sixth step is the period when individual children, to the best of their ability, face their life at kindergarten squarely.

Among these six steps, we can consider that the first step, which comes around April (the new school year), is the mentally unstable period for children; the second and third steps are the stable periods; the fourth, fifth, and sixth steps (after the summer vacation) are when individual children demonstrate their abilities.

Children's Mental Progress and the Use of Picture Books

In these six steps, it has been found to be very effective to use picture books in the development of children's abilities. That is, in the first step, when children are mentally insecure in the new environment, they can be made to feel at ease if they are provided picture books they are already familiar with at home. In addition, by reading such picture books aloud to groups of children, teachers can communicate with them. The reading aloud also helps the children feel secure by providing them with something in common.

As these children enter the second step, picture books give them an even greater sense of security; the books may remind them of past experiences before attending kindergarten. For instance, the book *Peekaboo*, written by Miyoko Matsutani with pictures by Yasuo Segawa and published by Dohshin-sha, is a good book for children to talk to and to play with by themselves. And by talking to the figures in the book, children can imagine playing with them. *The Curious Little Kitten* (originally copyrighted in 1956 by Bernadine Cook) shows the pictures in sequence from left to right, which helps children to follow the story very easily. As a result, just by following the pictures, these children will show interest in the book, reacting honestly to the story told. This particular book has pictures and uses only the simplest possible lines and expressions to tell a story, with selected dialogue. Thus, it is very suitable as teaching material for children in kindergarten.

In the third step of development, children expand their experiences and verify them through picture books. In the process, they come to have common understandings. Through such processes, they learn to enjoy the company of others in group situations. These children love to listen to old folktales from Japan and other countries. For example, *The Three Billy Goats Gruff* is one of many stories familiar to Japanese children.

Children in the third step also like to look at pictures and listen to stories of one's experiences such as *Swimmy* (copyright 1963 by Leo Lionni and published by Pantheon Books), which tells how to find the joy of group life. Many children will find the story interesting and easy to accept.

After the summer recess, through the fourth and the fifth steps (September to December), children begin to have deeper association with others through picture books. And while a sense of companionship grows among children in these steps of child development, a sense of competition with others is also created. Teachers can let the children find how to behave in group situations. They have a strong tendency to want to engage in group play with others. With proper guidance by teachers, they can develop group playing abilities based on their past experiences. At the same time, a sense of companionship develops among them as they try to divide the roles of each member of a group or the whole class to achieve common goals and to settle quarrels among themselves. And being able to adjust themselves to such developments, these children come to understand and enjoy the following stories:

The Selfish Monkey and the Good-Natured Crab

Old Japanese folklore story about a selfish monkey being forced by a group of crabs to reflect on his bad behavior.

The Little House by Virginia Lee Burton, Houghton Mifflin, 1942.

This American story centers on a small house in the country, which faces a danger of being destroyed for new and modern buildings. But, in the end, the people realize how important it is to keep traditional things in this age of modernization, and the small rural house survives in another rural area.

Die Bremer Stadtmusikanten (The Musicians of Bremen) copyright by Hans Fischer, 1948.

In this fairy tale by Jacob Grimm, aging animals work together, with their special talents, to get rid of a thief.

The Tree of Mochi Mochi, Japan Creative Picture Book, written by Ryusuke Saito with pictures by Jiro Takidaira, 1971. Printed in Japan.

A five year old boy named Mameta, who lives with his

hunter grandfather, is too cowardly to get up at night by himself to urinate. However, one evening when his beloved grandfather is dying, Mameta goes alone for a doctor to save his grandfather. And that night, Mameta sees the lighted tree of Mochi Mochi, which can only be seen by courageous children.

By the sixth step (January to March), children should understand the sentiment of picture books. They are already able to enjoy the basic stories of picture books in the fourth and fifth steps. And by this time of the school year, they can enter into the sentiments of characters in the picture book stories and discuss them with other children.

Children in the sixth step tend to enjoy games that arouse their intellectual interests. They also know what they want to do. And they seek to demonstrate their own abilities in a group—they may encourage their friends to join their play or to think up a new game; and by doing this, their groups, or the whole class, begin to act on their own initiative. In this step, the number of those interested in words and characters increases and you see children enjoying picture books by themselves. In addition, they find something in common with others. Their sentiments and facilities with speech are developed as well as their creativity and imagination; and with picture books they can confirm their own personal experiences, expand them, and gain new knowledge. As a result, they tend to prefer reading picture books that will take them to the world of imagination and fantasy.

Children in the sixth step should have picture books which give variety in substance, give thrills and the spirit of adventure, appeal to the emotions, and can be appreciated by the children who share the world of fantasy with their friends.

The First Errand, Japan Creative Picture Book, written by Yoriko Tsutsui with pictures by Meiko Hayaski.

A five year old girl is sent on her first errand by her mother to buy milk for her baby sister. She worries about her first errand, loses her money but is delighted to find it later, feels a bit ignored at the store because she is not tall enough to be noticed by the people behind the counter, but in the end she does the errand well. The girl feels a sense of accomplishment and satisfaction for the first time in her life after she gives the milk to her mother.

Mental and Attitude Changes of Five Year Old Children

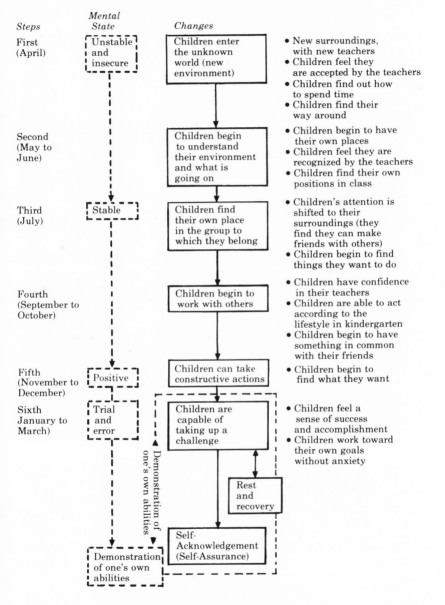

Steps	Mental State	Changes	
First (April)	Unstable and insecure	Children enter the unknown world (new environment)	• New surroundings, with new teachers • Children feel they are accepted by the teachers • Children find out how to spend time • Children find their way around
Second (May to June)		Children begin to understand their environment and what is going on	• Children begin to have their own places • Children feel they are recognized by the teachers • Children find their own positions in class
Third (July)	Stable	Children find their own place in the group to which they belong	• Children's attention is shifted to their surroundings (they find they can make friends with others) • Children begin to find things they want to do
Fourth (September to October)		Children begin to work with others	• Children have confidence in their teachers • Children are able to act according to the lifestyle in kindergarten • Children begin to have something in common with their friends
Fifth (November to December)	Positive	Children can take constructive actions	• Children begin to find what they want
Sixth January to March)	Trial and error	Children are capable of taking up a challenge	• Children feel a sense of success and accomplishment • Children work toward their own goals without anxiety

Rest and recovery

Self-Acknowledgement (Self-Assurance)

Demonstration of one's own abilities

Demonstration of one's own abilities

Suho's White Horse, a folklore story in Mongolia, retold by Yuzo Ohtsuka with pictures by Suekichi Akaba. Printed in Japan.

A boy shepherd named Suho lives in the Mongolian steppe. One day he sees a white horse and decides to look after the horse. But the horse is found by the king of Mongolia and taken away from the boy. The horse is killed while trying to flee to the boy master, and the Mongolian musical instrument—the harp with the head of a horse which is made of the horse's bones—is left with the boy. When he plays the harp, the beautiful melodies keep the villagers in peace.

The Book of A,I,U,E,O (Japanese Alphabet), pictures by Mitsuyoshi Anno. *Anno's Alphabet,* M. Anno, Crowell, 1975.

The book deals humorously with the characteristics in sound and shape of the 50 letters from A to N in the Japanese alphabet.

The Book of ABC, pictures by Mitsuyoshi Anno.

This is a fantasy picture book with each letter of the alphabet looking like a piece of wood. The author fills this book with his imagination and humor.

These picture books give proper guidance to the children in the sixth stage of development. The books satisfy the intellectual needs and interests of the children, enable them to develop and demonstrate their imaginations, and help them indulge themselves in their fantasy worlds.

Conclusion

Children go through constant mental development in group situations, in kindergarten or nursery school, by living with others. The use of picture books has proved to be very effective for the total growth of children as human beings.

And now we can select picture books which are superb in artistic quality and substantial in content. We can find such good picture books on a worldwide basis.

Encouraging the Reading Habit

Ralph C. Staiger
International Reading Association
Newark, Delaware
United States of America

Most of us believe that it is desirable that the reading habit be encouraged. We agree, in principle, but we may not agree on the details of stimulating children and adults to become habitual readers. For one thing, we recognize that, although we tend to want to create readers in our own image—readers interested in the same books and ideas as those we cherish—we know that individuals differ in their leanings and concerns, and we cannot realistically expect to create clones of our reading selves.

Unfortunately, teachers in the United States and many other countries have not taken much time for encouraging the reading habit. The norm appears to be that teachers spend so much energy imparting information that there is little time left for creating a love for books and reading. There are many exceptions, and it is significant that students, in their later years, remember those teachers who have pushed their frontiers back and who have forced them to become learners. Students quickly forget the knowledge-dispensers.

Why Do People Read?

Gray and Rogers (2) have presented a carefully compiled list of purposes for reading which suggests that the habit of using reading is based upon real human needs. Variations in motivation for reading may occur in various cultures throughout the world, but this list of purposes provides a useful foundation:

1. As a ritual, or from force of habit
2. From a sense of duty
3. To kill time
4. To know and understand current happenings
5. For immediate personal satisfaction or value—for fun, pleasure, escape
6. To further avocational interests—to learn about hobbies
7. To carry on and promote professional or vocational interests
8. To meet personal-social demands
9. To meet sociocivic needs and demands (good citizenship)
10. For self-development or improvement, including extension of cultural background
11. To satisfy intellectual demands
12. To satisfy spiritual needs

Lapsed readers offer many excuses for not reading. Radio and television have been blamed, as have "poor eyes," and "too much housework." One never knows the truth in all cases, and we can always find exceptions such as people with poor eyes who enjoy radio and television and those who do a lot of housework and also read a great deal.

Of the several case studies of mature readers included in the Gray and Rogers study, the individual who was most nearly mature in all areas (Case Y-3) was a professional woman, whose activity in civic affairs contributed to her breadth and depth of interests, as well as her purposes for reading. Her awareness of these purposes was outstanding, as were the intellectual challenge of the material read, the richness of ideas involved, and the varying difficulty of what she read. While some reading was at a level of great interest and penetration, some of it was at a superficial level—merely to satisfy a passing interest or whim. This was especially striking, for her schedule allowed little time to spend in reading. She did not use the frequently heard excuse that there was not enough time for reading.

Much later, in a quite different context, Kamarás (4) reported a similar finding. In spite of having less leisure time, Hungarian workers who were continuing their education were found to be reading greater quantities of material and also reading more often than those who were not continuing their schooling.

How Has Reading Been Encouraged in Various Countries?

During the past few decades, a number of organized attempts have been made to stimulate the reading of the general public. I would like to share a few of them with you, as they were described in a recent Unesco publication (5).

Several different approaches were taken. Some were directed at children of school age, others to the general adult population, and some to both.

New Zealand

As most people in the book world know, 1972 was celebrated as International Book Year, and national book councils were established in many countries. As an initial major undertaking, the New Zealand Book Council decided that it would engage in a project which has become known as "The Book Flood."

Many investigators were interested in why some children had become habitual readers and others had not. However, no sustained and systematic experiment had been conducted to test the assumption that reading tastes are likely to be influenced by the supply of books available. The New Zealand Department of Education, the School Library Service, and several advisory committees to plan the project in detail were also involved actively with the New Zealand Book Council.

With the assistance of the New Zealand Centre for Educational Research, the study was conducted in the city of Auckland, where two primary schools had been identified by local inspectors as having enrolled many children who had limited access to books. Large numbers of Polynesian children from varying language backgrounds were in these schools. There were few books in their classrooms, and the principals of the schools showed high interest in the project. Each school was to be supplied with 400-500 good books per classroom, from entering classes through the fourth standard, and the effects of this improved supply of books upon the reading habits, interests, and skills of children were assessed as well as the practices and views of the teachers. The experiments pointed out the significant fact that the stack of books brought the collections available to these schools up to the range and quality of books which were available in the most favored 10-15 percent of schools of similar size and type.

According to informal observation by teachers and visitors, the initial impact of the Book Flood was good. The children seemed enthusiastic about the unaccustomed range of attractive and interesting books; they spent more time reading and talking about books; they borrowed more books for home use and took books home for their parents to read. The investigators were not satisfied with these observations, however, for they do not tell us about the long term effects of books on children's behavior.

The Evaluation Committee selected and devised suitable tests, questionnaires, and rating scales. Initial baseline levels were obtained for reading comprehension, vocabulary, and listening skills; and a survey of reading interests was adapted to assess the children's interests in books and other reading materials. An attitude scale was used to assess the older children's attitudes toward school, reading, and themselves. The junior children's word recognition skills, letter identification, and familiarity with books and print were estimated with standardized tests, and teacher ratings on a three-point scale were used to assess the attitudes of the younger children. In addition, the teachers who participated made confidential assessments of their own practices and beliefs in the teaching of reading, using a checklist devised by the Evaluation Committee. All of these evaluations were made before the books were made available, so that follow-up comparisons could be made after the Book Flood had been in operation for some time.

An intensive case study was made of five children from each class. Questions were asked about books owned and read and about home background, parental interest, library borrowing, television viewing, and other factors likely to be influenced by the Book Flood. Studies were made of the children's reading behaviors, using informal reading inventories and running records.

From the baseline data, it was seen that, in the life of the typical child in these schools, books and reading played a very small part. Few children had favorite authors, and most had little access to books. The average number of children in the families represented in the study was five. The average child watched television for 22.5 hours per week, although some claimed over 47 hours of viewing. There were few books in the home, and in one school 81 percent claimed that their parents never read to them. In the other school, the proportion was 44 percent. More than half of the children never read a newspaper. The vast majority spoke English at home, but for many of them it was not their mother tongue.

One year later, additional measurements were taken, to ascertain the long term impact of the Book Flood. The children had more than doubled their reading as a result of the Flood. The reading and listening comprehension test results were very similar to those of an interim study. Listening comprehension improvement was the greatest, and the children, significantly in light of the nature of the group, held their own in the general skills measured by the reading tests. This is considered significant because children with language difficulties, and from depressed socioeconomic and cultural conditions, often lose ground rather than continue to gain, when compared with the general population. The Book Flood had marked effects during the first six months, and maintained these effects throughout the second year.

The teachers' views on the success of the experiment were varied, but the majority of the staff was confident that the project was successful in "hooking" many children on books. It is interesting to observe that those teachers who reported a decline in interest in the Book Flood also revealed that the impact of the program upon their own behavior had been minimal.

In the final paragraph of the evaluation, the success of the Book Flood was summarized: "In sum, the majority of teachers felt that availability of a rich supply of 300-400 well-chosen books per classroom was a very commendable policy, and while not the critical factor in bringing children to a lasting habit of reading, it was an important first step. Their opinions are supported, by and large, with the information that most children were consistently reading much more, that their reading and listening skills were slowly but steadily improving, and that they were becoming more familiar with books and authors" (1).

Significantly, the National Book League in the United Kingdom has embarked on a long term experiment along the same lines. The project is being funded by the British National Bibliography Research Fund Committee, is being monitored by Bradford University's Postgraduate School of Studies in Research in Education, and will be followed with interest.

Australia

An example of how a professional public relations firm can be used to promote a book week celebration is exemplified in the OZBOOKWEEK in Melbourne.

The main objective of the campaign was to reach the 65 percent of the Australian public who are not regular book purchasers. The public relations firm reported that OZBOOKWEEK was an unqualified success.

The broad objectives of the program were to sharpen awareness in the community of Australian books, to increase the instance and frequency of buying and borrowing of Australian books, to stimulate interest in Australian books, and to enhance the attitudes of the Australian public to Australian books.

The selection of an alternative name to Australian Book Week was not easy. Eventually the name OZBOOKWEEK was decided upon, as a memorable, different and informal title for this book week celebration. "OZ" was derived from a shortened version of "Australia" which appears to be accepted equally by the different groups of Australians, who were the target audience.

The promotional activities were tied to individual books by the use of an especially designed Australian book seal, which could be affixed to book covers and so specify that this was an Australian book. The design was also used in advertising, in general publicity, and in conjunction with display material of various kinds.

Newspapers were encouraged to run either enlarged book features or special supplements on books, which would help spread the message of OZBOOKWEEK. Each country newspaper was sent a package of at least twenty book reviews and additional editorial matter relating to Australian writing and publishing. These were published in twenty-four large and small newspapers, and it was estimated from reliable statistics that over four million readers saw the OZBOOKWEEK message at the beginning of the week.

In some places, special ceremonies inaugurating OZBOOKWEEK attracted a wider audience for the display and aroused interest in Australian books. Some booksellers bought space in local newspapers and used other media to draw attention to the displays. Press clippings submitted by the entrants indicated that the displays produced extensive editorial and pictorial coverage. Book lists of Australian books in the display were distributed and, in some cases, books borrowed from the local library or for sale at bookshops were made available. Added strength was gained through the involvement of many persons not connected with the book trade in the display competition. Display staff, children, and amateur photographers all participated enthusiastically. A librarian in a small high school wrote of the results, "I doubt that any of the 3,000 inhabitants of our Shire were not made aware of OZBOOKWEEK. Most of the students have been wholeheartedly behind this activity and they worked together as a team. Perhaps this competition has been one of the best things to encourage such school spirit" (3).

A costumed creature known as the Ozbookworm personified the celebration in many ways, and was seen by an estimated 24,000 persons. Ozbookworm presented the Lord Mayor of Melbourne with a special book at the opening ceremony, Liardet's *Water Colors of Old Melbourne.* In Sydney, an Ozbookworm appeared for five days, for about three minutes each day, in an excellent series of television appearances. Ozbookworm also appeared in department stores and city bookstores. A recommendation was made for a children's television series on the adventures of "Ozbookworm in Literature Land." The actors who portrayed the Ozbookworm reported that he created an instant audience with both young and old.

Many other opportunities to publicize Ozbookworm were taken all over Australia. In each of the six large cities, where the great majority of the country's population lives, activities such as radio and television interviews, special storytelling sessions, and dinners were held.

Japan

A trip on a Japanese railroad train will convince a foreigner that almost everyone in Japan reads. Yet, the Japanese say that their countrymen are not good book readers, and they have mounted numerous nationwide and local reading campaigns. This is a country with very high literacy!

For thirty years, a National Book Week has been sponsored by the Japan Council for the Promotion of Book Reading. Book Week actually lasts for two weeks and is held at the time of the Culture Day holiday, on November 3. Posters are distributed throughout the country by way of schools, libraries, bookstores, and similar agencies. Newspapers and magazines devote pages to reading promotion during this period. Outstanding people and groups who have made significant contributions to reading are given awards, and lectures or study meetings concerning book reading are held in many cities.

All of these activities are financed by the Japan Council for the Promotion of Book Reading, with which all publishers, newspapers, and booksellers are affiliated. One exception is a lottery, sponsored by the Japanese Association of Bookstores, which is designed to promote book buying. A ticket is given during this period for each purchase of a book costing more than 500 yen.

Also sponsored by the Japan Council, as well as some other groups associated with newspapers and mass communication, is an annual Children's National Book Week. Under this umbrella are conducted a wide range of activities which encourage children to read—children's book fairs, exhibitions of picture books from around the world, book report contests, and the wide distribution of a pamphlet recommending 100 good books for children.

The *doshuko Kanso-bun*, which can be literally translated as "reading-impression composition," is different from what is known as a "book report" in many cultures. Japanese children are encouraged to write their own views on the relationships between the theme of a book they have just read and their past and future lives, as well as summarizing the book and telling what they thought of it.

The nationwide contest, sponsored by the Mainichi Newspapers and the Japan School Library Association, is carried on at four levels: lower elementary, upper elementary, junior high school, and senior high school. About one million children enter the contest each year. The first prize winner at each level is awarded the "Prime Minister's Prize," and is given the honor of reading the report before the Imperial Family. This is an extremely creative use of the book report idea, and is a far cry from the pedantic use of book reports dreaded by children for many years.

The uniquely Japanese inclination toward group action can be seen in the development of cooperative libraries called "Bunko." Kyoko Matsuoka, the Director of the Tokyo Children's Library, described the growth of the Bunko effectively in an article which first appeared in the newsletter of the Unesco Regional Centre for Book Development in Karachi in April 1976.

A movement begun in 1960 by Natoju Muku in Kagoshima Prefecture has spread all over Japan. In this plan, children read aloud from a book for twenty minutes every day while their parents (usually their mothers) listen to them. This simple plan has the advantages of having the parent and child share the same feelings and obtain the same knowledge through reading a book. It is also effective in promoting the reading habit.

Another similar plan encourages mothers to read aloud to their infants and young children, even though little comprehension of what is read takes place. The psychological effect of such reading creates warmth and positive attitudes toward books and reading which are difficult to duplicate in later life.

Conclusion

One of the purposes of the International Reading Association is to develop an awareness of the impact of reading by encouraging the development of worthwhile reading tastes and permanent interests in reading, promoting the formation of lifetime habits of reading, and developing an appreciation of the value of reading in a democratic society.

We have a responsibility to go beyond the teaching of the skills of reading, beyond the setting of purposes for efficient reading, beyond the diagnosis of reading difficulties and the identification of miscues in reading not only because we are affiliated with the IRA, but because, as educated individuals, we are responsible for carrying on the heritage of our people.

References

1. ELLEY, W.B., C.R. COWIE, and J.E. WATSON. *The Impact of Book Flood.* Wellington, New Zealand: New Zealand Centre for Educational Research, 1975.
2. GRAY, WILLIAM S., and BERNICE ROGERS. *Maturity in Reading.* Chicago, Illinois: University of Chicago Press, 1956.
3. International Public Relations, Pty. Confidential Report to the National Book Council of Australia, 1967.
4. KAMARÁS, ISTVÁN. *Az Irodalmi Érték Esélye Lektürol Vasóknál.* Budapest: Nepmuvelesi Iroda, 1974.
5. STAIGER, RALPH C. *Roads to Reading.* Paris: Unesco, 1979.